I0840384

To God, for lighting my path; to my husband N.M., for his unwavering strength; and to my friend K.C., whose encouragement and support are invaluable, my deepest gratitude.

Ghelere Publishing

2024

This Book Belongs to:

ALL RIGHTS RESERVED
2024

No part of this publication may be reproduced, distributed, or transmitted in any form or by any means, including photocopying, recording, or other electronic or mechanical methods, without the prior written permission of the publisher, except for brief quotations incorporated in critical reviews and other specific noncommercial uses. Any unauthorized replica of this work is prohibited.

G.P. ©
all rights reserved

TYRANNOSAURUS REX

The T. rex, one of the largest terrestrial carnivores, was a top predator, feeding on large dinosaurs. An intriguing curiosity is that, despite its ridiculously small arms, they were extremely strong, capable of lifting hundreds of kilograms.

TYRANNOSAURUS REX

ACTIVITY: THE MIGHTY T-REX IN ACTION

CHALLENGE: DRAW A T-REX DOING WHAT IT DOES BEST.
- IS IT HUNTING, ROARING, OR PERHAPS SHOWING ITS SOFTER SIDE?

VELOCIRAPTOR

The Velociraptor, famous for its agility and intelligence, was a small carnivore that hunted in packs. Contrary to its popular portrayal, it was the size of a turkey and covered in feathers, a curiosity that strengthens its connection to modern birds.

VELOCIRAPTOR

ACTIVITY: THE STRATEGIC HUNT OF VELOCIRAPTOR

CHALLENGE: ILLUSTRATE A GROUP OF VELOCIRAPTORS WORKING TOGETHER ON A HUNT.
- HOW DO THEY COMMUNICATE AND PLAN THEIR STRATEGY?

TRICERATOPS

The Triceratops, with its large skull shield and three horns, was a herbivore that roamed in herds to protect itself from predators like the T. rex. A curiosity is that the horns and shield could also be used in displays to attract mates.

TRICERATOPS

ACTIVITY: THE HORN PARADE OF TRICERATOPS

CHALLENGE: CREATE A SCENE WHERE THE TRICERATOPS IS USING ITS HORNS.
- IS IT IN A DISPUTE, PROTECTING ITS FAMILY, OR JUST OUT FOR A STROLL?

THERIZINOSAURUS

The Therizinosaurus is unique for its enormous claws, the largest of any known dinosaur, which it used to pull down branches to feed. Despite its frightening appearance, it was herbivorous.

THERIZINOSAURUS

ACTIVITY: THE LONG CLAWS OF THERIZINOSAURUS

CHALLENGE: DRAW THE THERIZINOSAURUS WITH ITS HUGE CLAWS.
- IS IT REACHING FOR HIGH LEAVES OR DEFENDING ITS TERRITORY?

STEGOSAURUS

Famous for its rows of bony plates along its back and spikes on its tail, the Stegosaurus was herbivorous, feeding on ground plants. A curiosity is that, despite its large size, its brain was only the size of a walnut.

STEGOSAURUS

ACTIVITY: PLATES AND SPIKES OF STEGOSAURUS

CHALLENGE: ILLUSTRATE A STEGOSAURUS, FOCUSING ON ITS PLATES AND TAIL SPIKES.
- HOW DOES IT USE THESE FEATURES TO PROTECT ITSELF?

PTERANODON

Although not technically a dinosaur but a flying reptile, the Pteranodon fed on fish, catching them while flying low over bodies of water. A curiosity is that, despite its large wings, it likely spent a lot of time at sea, using its large rear limbs as rudders.

PTERANODON

ACTIVITY: THE MAJESTIC FLIGHT OF PTERANODON

CHALLENGE: CREATE A SCENE WITH THE PTERANODON FLYING OVER THE OCEAN.
- WHAT CAN IT CATCH WITH ITS BEAK?

MICRORAPTOR

The Microraptor was a small dinosaur with four wings, suggesting it could glide between trees. Its diet likely consisted of insects and small vertebrates. This dinosaur offers valuable insights into the evolution of flight in dinosaurs.

MICRORAPTOR

ACTIVITY: FLYING WITH THE MICRORAPTOR

CHALLENGE: IMAGINE AND DRAW THE MICRORAPTOR GLIDING BETWEEN TREES.
- WHAT DOES IT SEE FROM UP THERE?

KENTROSAURUS

The Kentrosaurus was a herbivore covered in spikes and bony plates. Smaller than its cousin, the Stegosaurus, it used its spikes for defense against predators. Interestingly, its spiky tail was extremely flexible, able to be swung like a whip.

KENTROSAURUS

ACTIVITY: THE SPIKY KENTROSAURUS

CHALLENGE: DRAW A KENTROSAURUS AND THINK ABOUT HOW ITS SPIKES PROTECT IT.
- IS IT IN A DEFENSIVE POSITION OR RELAXING?

IGUANODON

One of the first dinosaurs discovered the Iguanodon was herbivorous and had spike-like thumbs, used for defense or for foraging food. It was capable of walking on both two and four legs.

IGUANODON

ACTIVITY: THE USEFUL THUMBS OF IGUANODON

CHALLENGE: ILLUSTRATE AN IGUANODON USING ITS SPIKY THUMBS.
- IS IT DEFENDING ITSELF, FORAGING, OR GREETING ANOTHER DINOSAUR?

GIGANOTOSAURUS

Larger than the Tyrannosaurus Rex, the Giganotosaurus was a fearsome carnivore that hunted large herbivorous dinosaurs. A curiosity is that fossils suggest it might have hunted in groups, a rare strategy among large theropods.

GIGANOTOSAURUS

ACTIVITY: FIND THE GIGANOTOSAURUS

CHALLENGE: DRAW A GIGANOTOSAURUS AND SOME POSSIBLE HIDING SPOTS.
 • WHERE DOES IT LIKE TO REST OR WAIT FOR ITS PREY?

GALLIMIMUS

The Gallimimus, with an omnivorous diet, ran swiftly across the plains in search of insects, small animals, and vegetation. Its name means "chicken mimic," referring to its ability to run quickly on two legs.

GALLIMIMUS

ACTIVITY: THE FAST RACE OF GALLIMIMUS

CHALLENGE: DRAW A GALLIMIMUS RUNNING THROUGH THE PLAINS.
   • IS IT FLEEING OR PLAYING WITH OTHER GALLIMIMUS?

DIPLODOCUS

The Diplodocus, famous for its extremely long body, and whip-like tail, was herbivorous, feeding mainly on low-lying plants. Interestingly, its tail could produce a cracking sound when moved rapidly, possibly used as communication or to deter predators.

DIPLODOCUS

ACTIVITY: THE DEFENDER TAIL OF DIPLODOCUS

CHALLENGE: ILLUSTRATE HOW THE DIPLODOCUS USES ITS LONG TAIL TO DEFEND AGAINST A PREDATOR.
 • SHOW THE TAIL IN ACTION!

DILOPHOSAURUS

The Dilophosaurus is often remembered for its portrayal in movies, with distinctive crests and the fictional ability to spit poison. In reality, it was a large carnivore that hunted prey such as small dinosaurs and reptiles, using its powerful bite.

DILOPHOSAURUS

ACTIVITY:DECORATING THE CREST OF DILOPHOSAURUS

CHALLENGE: DRAW A DILOPHOSAURUS WITH ITS DISTINCTIVE CRESTS.
- HOW DO YOU IMAGINE THE COLORS AND PATTERNS OF THESE CRESTS?

COELOPHYSIS

One of the oldest known dinosaurs, the Coelophysis was a light and agile carnivore, hunting in packs to better capture its prey. A curiosity is that fossils suggest they may have practiced cannibalism in times of scarcity.

COELOPHYSIS

ACTIVITY: HUNTER FRIENDS COELOPHYSIS

CHALLENGE: CREATE A HUNTING SCENE WITH SEVERAL COELOPHYSIS.
- WHAT ARE THEY HUNTING TOGETHER IN THE FOREST?

COMPSOGNATHUS

The Compsognathus was small, not larger than a modern chicken, and fed on insects and other small animals. Its small stature and agility made it an effective hunter, capable of chasing quick prey through dense forests.

COMPSOGNATHUS

ACTIVITY: THE BIG SMALL WORLD OF COMPSOGNATHUS

CHALLENGE: DRAW A COMPSOGNATHUS AND THE SMALL WORLD AROUND IT FULL OF INSECTS AND PLANTS.
- WHAT DOES IT LIKE TO EAT?

CERATOSAURUS

The Ceratosaurus, a formidable predator, fed on a variety of prey, including fish, thanks to its sharp teeth and agile body. It had a large horn on its nose, which was likely used both for combat and for display.

CERATOSAURUS

ACTIVITY: THE HORN OF CERATOSAURUS

CHALLENGE: DRAW A CERATOSAURUS AND DECORATE ITS HORN UNIQUELY.
  • HOW DOES IT USE THIS HORN TO IMPRESS OR FIGHT?

CARNOTAURUS

The Carnotaurus was a carnivore with a pair of distinctive horns above its eyes, resembling a bull, hence its name. These horns might have been used in fights with other Carnotaurus. A peculiar feature was its skin, which exhibited unique textures, suggesting possible adaptations for thermoregulation or camouflage.

CARNOTAURUS

ACTIVITY: THE CARNOTAURUS RACE

CHALLENGE: IMAGINE A SCENE WHERE THE CARNOTAURUS IS RUNNING.
- WHAT IS IT CHASING? DRAW THE ENTIRE SCENE!

BRACHIOSAURUS

The Brachiosaurus was known for its extraordinarily long neck, which it used to reach leaves on tall trees, its primary food source. A curiosity is that, unlike many other long-necked dinosaurs, its front legs were longer than its rear ones, giving it a unique inclined posture.

BRACHIOSAURUS

ACTIVITY: REACH THE LEAVES WITH THE BRACHIOSAURUS

CHALLENGE: DRAW A BRACHIOSAURUS TRYING TO EAT LEAVES AT THE TOP OF A TREE.
- MAKE THE TREE REALLY TALL AND THE BRACHIOSAURUS STRETCHING ITS LONG NECK.

ANKYLOSAURUS

The Ankylosaurus, the living tank of the Cretaceous, was herbivorous, feeding on low-growing plants. Its most notable characteristic was the bony armor covering its entire body, including a large club on its tail, which it used to defend against predators.

ANKYLOSAURUS

ACTIVITY: CREATE ARMOR FOR THE ANKYLOSAURUS

CHALLENGE: DRAW AN ANKYLOSAURUS AND GIVE IT THE MOST AMAZING ARMOR YOU CAN IMAGINE.

ARGENTINOSAURUS

The Argentinosaurus, truly a colossus, was herbivorous, feeding on the tops of the tallest trees. It is estimated to have been one of the largest dinosaurs that ever existed with lengths that could reach 35 meters or more. Its enormity makes it a fascinating study in biomechanics.

ARGENTINOSAURUS

ACTIVITY: HOW TALL IS THE ARGENTINOSAURUS?

CHALLENGE: DRAW AN ARGENTINOSAURUS AND NEXT TO IT, PLACE OBJECTS OR ANIMALS TO SHOW HOW GIGANTIC IT IS. USE YOUR CREATIVITY!

ALLOSAURUS

The Allosaurus, a fearsome predator, roamed the Jurassic lands in search of its next meal. A fierce carnivore, it primarily feasted on smaller dinosaurs and large reptiles. An impressive curiosity is that Allosaurus had relatively large and strong arms for its size, with sharp claws, used to grasp prey before the final kill.

ALLOSAURUS

ACTIVITY: DRAW THE ALLOSAURUS' DINNER

CHALLENGE: IMAGINE AND DRAW WHAT YOU THINK THE ALLOSAURUS WOULD LIKE TO EAT. IT COULD BE ANYTHING FROM SMALL DINOSAURS TO LARGE REPTILES!

APATOSAURUS

This gentle giant, the Apatosaurus, was one of the largest dinosaurs to ever walk the Earth. With a strictly herbivorous diet, it consumed massive amounts of vegetation to sustain its immense size. A curiosity is that, despite its long neck, research suggests it probably did not lift it very high.

APATOSAURUS

ACTIVITY: THE APATOSAURUS BUFFET

CHALLENGE: DRAW AN APATOSAURUS AND AROUND IT, DRAW ALL THE DELICIOUS PLANTS AND TREES IT MIGHT WANT TO EAT.

GHELERE PUBLISHING

www.ingramcontent.com/pod-product-compliance
Lightning Source LLC
Chambersburg PA
CBHW081023260726
48662CB00026B/2969